Crypto Essentials Book Three

Getting Started with Trading and Investing Cryptocurrencies

Scott Jenkins

Disclaimer

The information contained in this book is provided for educational and informational purposes only. While every effort has been made to ensure that the information provided is accurate and up to date, the author makes no warranties, either express or implied, regarding the completeness, reliability, or accuracy of the content.

Readers should not rely solely on the information provided in this book when making financial, legal, or investment decisions. The content is not intended to serve as professional advice and should not replace consultation with a licensed expert in fields such as financial planning, investing, law, or any other professional services.

By using the information contained in this book, the reader agrees that the author is not liable for any losses, damages, or inconveniences incurred either directly or indirectly, as a result of the use or misuse of the content provided, including but not limited to errors, omissions, or inaccuracies.

Always do your own research and consult with a qualified professional before making any decisions based on the information in this book. Cryptocurrency markets are volatile and involve significant risk, and individual results may vary.

Contents

Introduction

IN 2013, A YOUNG programmer named Erik Finman made a bold decision that would forever change his financial future. At just 12 years old, he invested $1,000 — money gifted to him by his grandmother — into Bitcoin when each coin was priced at about $12. By 2017, his investment had ballooned into a million-dollar fortune. Erik's story is not only one of financial success but also a testament to the power of cryptocurrency to open doors for people who may not have had access to traditional forms of wealth generation.

Yet, for every success story like Erik's, there are countless others who struggle to navigate the complex world of cryptocurrency. Newcomers are often overwhelmed with jargon, confused by the endless options of exchanges and wallets, or simply paralyzed by the fear of losing money. This is where *Crypto Essentials Book Three: Getting Started with Trading and Investing in Cryptocurrencies* comes into play. I've created this book to provide you with a clear, practical roadmap to confidently start your journey in the world of crypto, without the frustration or fear that so many face.

Building on the Foundation: A Recap

Before diving into the actionable steps of getting started with crypto trading and investing, it's important to acknowledge the solid foundation already established in the first two books of the *Crypto Essentials* series. In *Crypto Essentials Book One: Understanding the Fundamentals of Cryptocurrencies and Blockchain Technology*, we laid out the basics of what cryptocurrency is, how it works, and why it's rapidly becoming a cornerstone of the future financial landscape. The first book was designed for absolute beginners, offering a clear definition of cryptocurrency, an overview of blockchain technology, and insights into leading cryptocurrencies and their use cases. It served as a gateway to understanding the fundamental concepts behind the crypto world and its comparison to traditional fiat money.

Building on that foundation, *Crypto Essentials Book Two: A Comprehensive Guide to the Acronyms and Key Terms* tackled the often-overwhelming jargon associated with cryptocurrency. The second book helped readers decode the buzzwords, acronyms, and key terms that are essential to navigating the crypto space. From understanding blockchain infrastructure and consensus models to diving into concepts like decentralized finance (DeFi), smart contracts, and non-fungible tokens (NFTs), this book ensured readers could confidently engage with the terminology of the crypto ecosystem.

Now, in *Crypto Essentials Book Three: Getting Started with Trading and Investing Cryptocurrencies*, we move from understanding the concepts to taking practical steps. This book is for those who are ready to take action, offering step-by-step guidance on how to start trading or investing in cryptocurrency. We may not revisit the basics already covered in the first two books except for a few mentions here and there where necessary. This book will focus on empowering you to set up accounts, make your first purchases, and start exploring the world of crypto with confidence. If you are interested to learn more of the fundamentals, I encourage you to scan the QR codes below to access the first two books in this series.

Scan for Crypto Essentials Book One

Scan for Crypto Essentials Book Two

If you've already read the previous books, you're well-prepared to dive into the practical aspects of getting started. And if this is your first encounter with the *Crypto Essentials* series, you'll find that this book stands on its own as a comprehensive, action-oriented guide to taking your first steps in the crypto world.

Key Benefits of Crypto

Before we delve into the practicalities, let's remind ourselves why people are increasingly turning to cryptocurrencies as a vehicle for financial growth. The crypto space offers several distinct advantages:

1. **Ownership and Control**: In the world of cryptocurrency, you own your assets directly, without needing to trust intermediaries like banks or financial institutions. This autonomy is one of the most empowering aspects of the crypto ecosystem.

2. **Global Access**: Crypto breaks down borders. Whether you're in New York or Nairobi, you can access the same financial opportunities, often with fewer barriers than traditional finance.

3. **Diversification**: Cryptocurrencies allow for diversification in ways that were previously inaccessible. Whether it's Bitcoin, Ethereum, or the rapidly expanding world of decentralized finance (DeFi), crypto opens new doors to expand your financial portfolio.

4. **Potential for High Returns**: While risk is inherent in any investment, crypto has proven to offer substantial returns for those who invest wisely. Bitcoin, for example, has grown exponentially

in value over the last decade, outperforming most traditional assets like stocks or bonds.

What This Book Will Teach You

This book isn't about theoretical knowledge; it's about giving you the tools to *get started*. Here's what we'll cover:

- **Choosing the Right Crypto Exchange**: We'll help you sift through the noise and identify the exchanges that are reputable, secure, and beginner-friendly.

- **Setting Up Your First Wallet**: From hot wallets to cold wallets, we'll guide you through the process of creating a secure place to store your digital assets.

- **Making Your First Purchase**: You'll learn how to buy your first cryptocurrency with confidence, and understand how to place different types of orders.

- **Risk Management**: No venture into crypto should be without a plan to manage risk. We'll cover essential strategies to protect your investments and minimize potential losses.

- **Tracking and Growing Your Portfolio**: Once you've bought your crypto, what's next? We'll introduce tools and methods to help you track your investments, avoid pitfalls, and grow your portfolio steadily.

By the time you finish this book, you'll have not only the knowledge but also the *confidence* to make informed decisions and take the first steps in your cryptocurrency journey. Our goal is to make sure that when you enter the market, you do so with a clear understanding of what to expect and how to navigate the process safely.

This book is practical, actionable, and designed for those ready to move from *curiosity* to *action*. Let's get started.

Chapter One

The Basics of Trading and Investing in Crypto

Entering the world of cryptocurrency requires understanding the key differences between trading and investing, as well as the strategies each entails. In this chapter, we'll explore both approaches, providing you with the foundational knowledge to make informed decisions as you begin your crypto journey.

Trading vs. Investing

When it comes to entering the world of cryptocurrency, one of the first decisions you need to make is whether you want to be a trader or an investor. While these terms are often used interchangeably, they represent two distinct approaches to engaging with the crypto market. Traders focus on short-term gains, often buying and selling cryptocurrencies within hours or days, taking advantage of the market's notorious volatility. Investors, on the other hand, take a longer-term approach, buying cryptocurrency with the intention of holding it for months or even years, waiting for the value to appreciate over time.

Before diving into either approach, it's crucial to understand the differences between these two methods. Each comes with its own set of strategies, risks, and potential rewards.

Trading: What is Crypto trading?

Crypto trading involves buying and selling cryptocurrencies over shorter periods to take advantage of rapid price movements. The goal of a trader is to "buy low, sell high" within a short time frame, whether that means hours, days, or weeks.

The fast pace of trading can be exhilarating, but it also demands a deep understanding of the market, quick decision-making, and the ability to manage risk effectively. Unlike traditional stock trading, where markets have set hours, crypto trading is a 24/7 activity. This means traders have constant opportunities to capitalize on price fluctuations, but it also requires vigilance.

Types of Crypto Traders

1. **Day Traders**: These traders buy and sell cryptocurrencies within the same day, aiming to take advantage of small price movements. Day trading

requires intense focus and a deep understanding of market signals, as price movements can be highly volatile in short time frames.

2. **Swing Traders**: Rather than executing multiple trades in a day, swing traders aim to capitalize on price "swings" that occur over days or weeks. This approach doesn't require the same constant attention as day trading but still demands a good understanding of market patterns and trends.

3. **Scalpers**: Scalping is a more intense form of trading that focuses on making small profits from numerous trades throughout the day. Scalpers may execute dozens or even hundreds of trades in a single day, hoping to benefit from tiny price movements.

Trading Strategies for Beginners

1. **Trend Following**: One of the most basic strategies for beginner traders is trend following. This involves identifying an overall upward (bullish) or downward (bearish) trend in the market and

executing trades in line with that trend. The idea is simple: go with the flow. If prices are rising, buy. If they're falling, sell.

2. **Breakout Trading**: A breakout occurs when the price moves beyond a defined support or resistance level. Breakout traders look for these critical moments when prices "break out" of a pattern, often signaling the start of a new trend.

3. **Range Trading**: For those who want to take a more measured approach, range trading involves buying when prices hit a low point in a predefined range and selling when they hit the high point. This strategy assumes that prices will continue to bounce between these levels for a time.

Tools for Crypto Trading

As a trader, you'll need to rely on certain tools to track the market and execute your trades efficiently:

1. **Candlestick Charts**: These charts provide detailed information about price movements in a given period (minutes, hours, days). They help

traders visualize the opening, closing, high, and low prices of an asset, making it easier to spot trends and predict movements.

2. **Order Types**: Understanding different types of orders (market, limit, stop-loss) is essential for executing your trades at the right moment. For example, a limit order allows you to specify a price at which you want to buy or sell an asset, giving you more control over the transaction.

3. **Indicators and Oscillators**: Tools like the Relative Strength Index (RSI) or Moving Averages help traders predict price movements based on historical data. These tools can assist you in identifying whether an asset is overbought or oversold, giving you insights into potential price reversals.

Investing: A Long-Term Approach

Unlike trading, investing in cryptocurrency is about playing the long game. Investors believe in the long-term potential of the asset and are willing to hold it for extended periods, regardless of short-term market fluctuations. The key to successful investing is patience and a belief that the asset will appreciate over time.

Investors often look at the fundamentals of a cryptocurrency: What problem does it solve? Who is behind the project? How large is its community? These questions help investors determine whether a coin has staying power.

Types of Crypto Investors

1. **HODLers**: The term "HODL" originated from a typo in an online forum, but it has since evolved into a popular strategy. HODLers are investors who buy cryptocurrency and hold onto it for years, even through periods of extreme volatility,

with the belief that the value will increase significantly in the long run.

2. **Value Investors**: Value investors, similar to those in traditional markets, look for coins or tokens they believe are undervalued. This involves researching a cryptocurrency's fundamentals and buying it when they feel it is trading below its intrinsic value.

3. **Income Investors**: These investors aren't just holding coins; they are also participating in decentralized finance (DeFi) projects like staking or yield farming to earn passive income from their investments.

Investment Strategies for Beginners

1. **Buy and Hold**: This is the simplest and most popular strategy among investors. It involves buying a cryptocurrency and holding onto it for an extended period, waiting for it to appreciate in value. It requires less effort and time than trading, but it still demands research to identify promising

cryptocurrencies.

2. **Dollar-Cost Averaging (DCA)**: Instead of trying to time the market, DCA involves buying small amounts of cryptocurrency at regular intervals, regardless of price. This strategy reduces the risk of entering the market at a high point and allows you to spread out your investment over time.

3. **Diversification**: Just as with any investment portfolio, it is essential not to put all your eggs in one basket. Diversifying across different cryptocurrencies helps reduce the risk of loss if one asset performs poorly.

Tools for Crypto Investing

Investors also rely on tools to track the progress of their investments and make informed decisions:

1. **Portfolio Trackers**: Tools like CoinGecko or CoinMarketCap allow investors to track their portfolios in real time, monitor the performance of various coins, and stay updated on market

trends.

2. **Fundamental Analysis Tools**: Unlike traders who focus on price charts, investors look at fundamentals. Websites like Messari or Glassnode provide in-depth reports and data on various blockchain projects, to help investors make informed decisions.

Short-Term vs. Long-Term Strategies

Now that you understand the difference between trading and investing, the next question is: Which strategy is best for you?

Short-Term Strategies (Trading)

- **Pros**: Traders can capitalize on price movements and potentially make quick profits. The ability to execute numerous trades provides flexibility.
- **Cons**: The crypto market's volatility makes trad-

ing risky. You can lose money quickly if you're not vigilant or don't have a well-developed strategy.

Long-Term Strategies (Investing)

- **Pros**: Investors have the advantage of riding out market fluctuations, which can help them avoid panic selling during price drops. Investing also requires less time than trading, making it ideal for those with other commitments.
- **Cons**: Long-term investing can be frustrating, especially in a market as volatile as cryptocurrency. It requires patience, and there's always the risk that a coin may not appreciate as expected.

Active vs. Passive Approaches

Your strategy will also depend on whether you prefer an active or passive approach. Active traders are more involved in the day-to-day movements of the market, while passive investors are content to set their investments and forget about them, checking in only occasionally.

- **Active**: Requires constant monitoring of the market and a readiness to react to price movements. If you enjoy researching and staying on top of trends, this could be for you.

- **Passive**: A more hands-off approach, ideal for people who want to invest without the stress of daily market fluctuations. A solid passive strategy can involve dollar-cost averaging and diversification across several assets.

Understanding Market Sentiment

One key factor that affects both trading and investing is market sentiment. Market sentiment refers to the overall attitude of investors and traders towards a particular asset or the market as a whole. In the crypto world, sentiment can swing wildly from one extreme to another, as has been seen with events like Bitcoin's meteoric rise in 2017 and its subsequent crash.

Understanding how market sentiment impacts price movements can help you make informed decisions. When sentiment is high (bull markets), prices tend to rise: when sentiment is low (bear markets), prices often fall. Staying in tune with the market's mood can give you an edge.

Bull and Bear Markets: Understanding Market Cycles

When you start trading or investing in cryptocurrency, two terms you'll soon come across are bull market and bear market. These terms describe the overall mood and momentum of many financial markets, including crypto. Understanding these cycles is crucial because they will influence your strategy, whether you are trading or investing.

1. **Bull Market**: A bull market refers to a period in which prices are rising or are expected to rise. This is typically fueled by investor confidence, strong demand, and a growing economy or favorable market conditions. In a bull market, you'll often see prices reaching new highs, and traders and investors feel optimistic. This is usually the best time for investors to buy and hold or for traders to ride the upward momentum for profits.

    - Example in Crypto: One of the most famous crypto bull markets happened between late 2020 and early 2021, where Bitcoin surged from $10,000 to over $60,000, leading the entire market into a massive upward trend.

2. **Bear Market**: On the other hand, a bear market is when prices are falling, and the sentiment is generally pessimistic. In this market, investors often panic sell, which can further drive prices down.

Bear markets are seen as the "winter" of financial markets, and many investors lose confidence. However, bear markets can also present buying opportunities, especially for long-term investors who see value in discounted assets.

- **Example in Crypto**: The most well-known crypto bear market occurred after the 2017 Bitcoin peak when prices dropped from nearly $20,000 to below $4,000 in just over a year. The entire market followed suit, with most cryptocurrencies losing significant value during this period.

What Should You Do in Bull and Bear Markets?

- In a bull market, traders often seek to capitalize on the momentum by buying dips and riding the upward trend. Investors may also hold their positions, waiting for higher returns as the market climbs.

- In a bear market, cautious traders might take short positions (betting on price decreases), while long-term investors might look to buy at lower prices, holding for when the market rebounds.

Understanding these cycles helps you make informed decisions about when to buy, sell, or hold your cryptocurrency. No market stays bullish or bearish forever, so being aware of these phases allows you to plan your moves accordingly.

Volatility in Crypto vs. Traditional Assets

One of the defining features of cryptocurrency markets is their volatility. Compared to traditional assets like stocks or bonds, crypto prices can swing dramatically over a short period. While this volatility offers traders opportunities to make quick gains, it also introduces significant risk.

1. **Crypto Volatility**: Cryptocurrencies are still relatively new, and their markets are more speculative, which is why you'll often see daily price swings of 5-10% or more. In extreme cases, some

altcoins have experienced fluctuations of over 50% in a single day. The lack of regulation, low liquidity in some markets, and the influence of social media or news events can all contribute to this high level of volatility.

- **Example**: In May 2021, a single tweet from Elon Musk stating that Tesla would no longer accept Bitcoin due to environmental concerns caused Bitcoin's price to plummet by 10% in just a few hours. The broader market also followed, leading to billions of dollars being wiped off the crypto market's value.

2. **Traditional Asset Volatility**: Traditional assets like stocks, bonds, and commodities tend to be much less volatile. While stock markets do experience significant movements during times of economic uncertainty, the day-to-day price swings are typically smaller and more predictable than in the crypto market. Governments and regulatory bodies closely monitor and manage these markets, which helps to stabilize them.

- **Example**: During a volatile period like the

2008 financial crisis, stocks experienced significant declines, but this was stretched over months and years rather than hours or days, making the traditional markets feel more predictable and less stressful for long-term investors.

Why Is Crypto So Volatile?

Several factors contribute to cryptocurrency's high volatility:

- **Market Maturity**: Cryptocurrencies are still relatively new compared to stocks which have been around for centuries. This means the market is more susceptible to speculation, panic, and extreme optimism.

- **Market Size**: The crypto market is smaller in terms of total value compared to traditional financial markets. This means even a large order or a big sell-off can significantly impact prices.

- **External Influences**: News events, regulatory announcements, or social media trends can cause sudden and massive price swings in crypto, which are not typically seen in traditional markets.

- **Liquidity**: Many smaller cryptocurrencies (altcoins) have low liquidity, meaning that they are not traded as frequently or in large volumes, making their prices more prone to sudden jumps or drops when larger orders come through.

Managing Volatility

For beginners, volatility might seem intimidating, but it's important to remember that volatility also creates opportunities. Here are a few strategies to manage volatility:

- **Diversify Your Portfolio**: Don't put all your funds into one cryptocurrency. By spreading your investments across multiple coins, you reduce the risk of one coin's volatility wiping out your portfolio.

- **Use Stop-Loss Orders**: When trading, you can use stop-loss orders to automatically sell your position if the price drops below a certain point. This helps to limit potential losses during periods of extreme volatility.

- **Consider Dollar-Cost Averaging**: Instead of trying to time the market perfectly, many investors use dollar-cost averaging (DCA), meaning they invest a fixed amount regularly. This smooths out the effects of volatility and allows them to accumulate crypto over time, regardless of short-term price swings.

Mastering Market Movements and Volatility

By understanding the concepts of bull and bear markets, you can better anticipate how the market might behave and develop strategies that align with your goals. Meanwhile, knowing how to manage the volatility of cryptocurrency markets will help you stay calm and make more informed decisions, rather than reacting emotionally to short-term price swings.

In this chapter, we've covered the basics of trading and investing in cryptocurrency. Whether you're drawn to the fast-paced world of trading or the long-term strategy of investing, both approaches have their advantages and risks. The key is finding a method that suits your personal goals, risk tolerance, and time commitment.

Now that you've learned about key market dynamics, you are ready to learn more about the practical aspects of getting started.

In the next chapter, we'll dive into the practical steps of setting up your first crypto account, so you can start your journey of trading or investing with confidence.

Chapter Two

Setting Up Your First Crypto Account

So, you've decided to take the plunge into the world of cryptocurrency? Awesome! But before you can start buying, selling, or trading your favorite coins, you need to set up your first crypto account. It's like getting your ticket to the crypto world. But with so many exchanges, security considerations, and account setup steps, it can feel a little overwhelming.

Don't worry — we've got you covered. This chapter will walk you through everything you need to know, from choosing the right exchange to securing your account. By the end, you'll be fully set up and ready to start your crypto journey!

How to Choose a Crypto Exchange

The first step in getting started with cryptocurrency is to choose the right crypto exchange. Think of an exchange as the marketplace where you'll be buying, selling, and trading your digital assets. But not all exchanges are created equal. There are many options out there, and the best one for you will depend on factors such as fees, security, and the type of coins you want to trade.

Here's what you need to look for when choosing your first crypto exchange:

1. **Fees**: Some exchanges charge higher fees than others. These fees can come in the form of trading fees, withdrawal fees, or deposit fees. It's important to understand how much each trade will cost you, as this can eat into your profits if you're not careful.

2. **Security**: One of the most important factors

when choosing an exchange is security. Look for exchanges with a strong reputation for protecting user funds. Features such as two-factor authentication (2FA), cold storage for funds, and insurance can provide an added layer of security.

3. **Regulation**: While cryptocurrencies operate outside the control of most governments, exchanges often need to comply with local regulations. Make sure the exchange you choose follows the laws in your country and has a track record of trustworthiness.

4. **Liquidity**: Liquidity refers to how easily you can buy or sell an asset without affecting its price. The more liquid an exchange is, the easier it will be to trade popular coins like Bitcoin or Ethereum. This is especially important if you plan on trading frequently.

5. **Coin Availability**: Not all exchanges offer every cryptocurrency. Some focus on popular coins like Bitcoin and Ethereum, while others offer a wide range of altcoins. If you are interested in exploring beyond the major players, make sure the exchange

you choose supports the coins you want to trade.

Popular Exchanges for Beginners

Now that you know what to look for, let's explore some of the most popular exchanges that are beginner-friendly:

1. **Binance**: Binance is one of the largest and most popular cryptocurrency exchanges in the world. It offers a wide variety of coins, low trading fees, and advanced security features. If you're interested in trading altcoins or diving deep into the crypto market, Binance is a great option.

2. **Coinbase**: For those just starting out, Coinbase is a favorite. It is known for being user-friendly and perfect for beginners. With an intuitive interface and a high level of security, Coinbase makes it easy to buy, sell, and store cryptocurrencies like Bitcoin and Ethereum. The downside? Fees can be higher than other exchanges.

3. **Kraken**: Kraken is another well-established exchange that offers a broad range of coins and advanced trading features. It is also known for its strong security and regulatory compliance, making it a solid option for those looking to trade safely.

4. **Gemini**: Gemini is a US-based exchange with a strong focus on security and regulation. While it doesn't offer as many coins as Binance or Kraken, it's a good option for those who prioritize safety and legal compliance.

Step-by-Step Guide to Creating an Account

Once you've chosen an exchange, it's time to create your account. Here's a step-by-step guide to help you get started:

1. **Sign Up**: Head over to the website of the exchange you've chosen and look for the "Sign Up" or "Register" button. You'll be prompted to enter

your email address and create a password.

- ***Pro Tip:*** *Make sure your password is strong—use a combination of uppercase letters, lowercase letters, numbers, and symbols. Avoid using common words or easily guessable information.*

2. **Email Verification**: After creating your account, the exchange will send a verification email to the address you provided. Check your inbox and follow the instructions in the email to verify your account.

3. **Enable Two-Factor Authentication (2FA)**: Security should be your top priority when dealing with cryptocurrency. Most exchanges offer two-factor authentication (2FA) as an extra layer of protection. This means you'll need to verify your identity using a second method (usually an app like Google Authenticator or a text message) whenever you log in or make a withdrawal.

    - Why This Matters: 2FA drastically reduces the chances of someone else accessing your account, even if they have your password.

4. **Complete KYC Verification**: Many exchanges require Know Your Customer (KYC) verification before you can start trading. This is a process where you'll provide personal information (such as your name, address, and date of birth) and upload documents (like a passport or driver's license) to verify your identity.
   - Don't Panic: This is a standard process, especially on regulated exchanges, and helps prevent fraud and money laundering. Make sure to provide accurate information to avoid delays.
5. **Deposit Funds**: Once your account is set up and verified, you'll need to deposit funds. Most exchanges allow you to deposit fiat currency (like USD, EUR, or GBP) using a bank transfer, credit card, or debit card. Some may also support other payment methods like PayPal or wire transfers.
   - Watch Out for Fees: Different deposit methods may have different fees. For example, cred-

it card deposits might come with higher fees compared to a bank transfer.

6. **Set Up Your Profile**: Many exchanges allow you to customize your account settings. Take a moment to explore your profile settings and update your notification preferences, security settings, and any other available options to enhance your user experience.

How to Keep Your Funds Safe

Cryptocurrency is exciting, but it also comes with risks—especially if you're not careful about security. Here are some best practices to follow to keep your funds safe:

1. **Use Strong Passwords**: As mentioned earlier, your password is your first line of defense. Make it strong and avoid reusing passwords across different platforms.

2. **Enable 2FA**: We can't stress this enough—always enable two-factor authentication. This simple step can go a long way in protecting your ac-

count.

3. **Beware of Phishing Scams**: Phishing scams are one of the most common ways people get tricked into giving away their crypto. Always double-check the URLs you visit and be cautious of any emails or messages asking for your login details.

4. **Cold Storage**: For large amounts of cryptocurrency, consider moving your funds to cold storage (offline storage) instead of keeping them on the exchange. This reduces the risk of hacking since cold wallets aren't connected to the internet.

Why You Need to "Know Your Customer"

KYC might feel like a hassle, but it is a critical part of the cryptocurrency landscape. Let's break it down:

- **What is KYC?** KYC is a regulatory process used by financial institutions (including crypto exchanges) to verify the identity of their users. It is designed to prevent illegal activities like money laundering, fraud, and terrorist financing.

- **Why is it Required?** Many countries have strict regulations regarding cryptocurrency, and exchanges need to comply with these laws. By completing KYC, you are helping the exchange to ensure all transactions are legitimate.
- **How Long Does It Take?** KYC verification can take anywhere from a few hours to a few days, depending on the exchange. To avoid delays, make sure you provide accurate information and high-quality scans of your documents.

By now, you should have your first crypto account fully set up and secured, ready for action. You've chosen the right exchange, gone through the KYC process, and taken steps to protect your funds. Now, you're all set to start buying your first cryptocurrency, which we will cover in the next chapter.

Congratulations on making it this far—you're well on your way to becoming a confident participant in the world of crypto!

Chapter Three

How to Buy Your First Crypto

YOUR FIRST CRYPTO PURCHASE is actually easier than you think, but before we launch out on this subject. Let me say this to you; "Congratulations! You've made it this far." Now comes the moment you've been waiting for — buying your first cryptocurrency. This can be an exciting but also nerve-wracking step. But don't worry. With the right tools and a clear understanding of the process, it's much easier than you may think.

In this chapter, we'll walk you through the methods available to purchase crypto using your regular money (called fiat). We'll cover different types of orders, how to pick a cryptocurrency to buy, and what you need to know about fees and best practices to ensure your first crypto transaction goes smoothly.

Fiat-to-Crypto On-Ramps

Before you can buy any crypto, you'll need to convert your fiat currency — whether it's USD, GBP, EUR, or another national currency — into cryptocurrency. This is done through a process called fiat-to-crypto on-ramps.

Here's how to do it:

Deposit Fiat on a Crypto Exchange

- The first and most common method is to deposit your fiat currency directly into your crypto exchange account. Most exchanges allow you to transfer funds via:

    - **Bank Transfer**: The most common and typically the cheapest method, though it may take a few days for the funds to appear in your exchange account.

    - **Credit/Debit Card**: A quicker option, but usually comes with higher fees (between 2% and 5%).

- ◦ **Third-Party Payment Services**: Some exchanges also allow PayPal, Apple Pay, or other payment services, but these often come with additional processing fees.
    - ***Pro Tip**: Check the fees before making a deposit. While bank transfers are often cheaper, the speed of using a card may be worth it if you're in a hurry.*

Using Fiat-Crypto Gateways

Some exchanges, like Coinbase or Binance, act as fiat-crypto gateways. These platforms allow you to purchase cryptocurrency directly using your credit card or bank account without needing to fund your exchange account separately. This method is quick and user-friendly, but it typically comes with higher transaction fees.

Understanding Market, Limit, and Stop-Limit Orders

Once your fiat currency is deposited into the exchange, it's time to buy your first cryptocurrency! But before you hit that "Buy" button, you'll need to understand the different types of orders you can place. Each type gives you more control over how and when your purchase is made.

1. **Market Order**: This is the simplest type of order. A market order executes immediately at the current market price. It's great for when you want to buy crypto quickly, but the downside is that you might pay a slightly higher price during periods of high volatility.
    - Best for: Beginners who want to make an immediate purchase without worrying about price fluctuations.
2. **Limit Order**: With a limit order, you set a specific price at which you want to buy a cryptocurrency. The order will only be executed when the price drops to or below your specified price. While this gives you control over the price you pay, it also means your order may not be filled if the price doesn't reach your target.
    - Best for: Those who are willing to wait for the right price and want to avoid overpaying during volatile market swings.

3. **Stop-Limit Order**: This is an advanced order type that combines a stop price with a limit price. Once the stop price is reached, the order becomes a limit order and will only be executed at or better than your limit price. This is often used for risk management when selling but can also be useful for buying during rapid price movements.
    - Best for: More experienced users who want precision in executing trades during volatile periods.

How to Evaluate a Coin or Token

While Bitcoin and Ethereum are great starting points, there's a vast world of altcoins (alternative cryptocurrencies) out there. But not all coins are created equal. Before buying any cryptocurrency, it's essential to evaluate its long-term potential. Here are a few factors to consider:

1. **Use Case**: What problem does the cryptocurrency solve? A good coin should have a strong use

case that differentiates it from others. For example, Ethereum's smart contracts enable decentralized applications, making it more than just a digital currency.

2. **Development Team**: Who is behind the project? A strong development team with a good track record can be a good sign that the project is legitimate and has long-term potential. Look for teams that are active and transparent about their progress.

3. **Partnerships**: Does the cryptocurrency have strong partnerships with other companies or projects? Partnerships can help a project gain more exposure and credibility.

4. **Community and Adoption**: How active is the community around the coin? A strong, engaged community often indicates widespread interest and adoption, which can drive a coin's value higher.

5. **Market Capitalization**: What is the total market cap of the coin? A higher market cap often

means a more stable and established cryptocurrency. Be cautious of coins with extremely low market caps, as they tend to be more volatile and risky.

Transaction Fees: What You Need to Know

Every time you make a cryptocurrency transaction, you'll encounter transaction fees. These fees vary depending on the exchange and the cryptocurrency being traded.

1. **Network Fees**: These fees go to miners or validators who process transactions on the blockchain. Bitcoin and Ethereum, for example, have network fees that fluctuate based on network activity and demand. High traffic can lead to higher fees.

2. **Exchange Fees**: Exchanges charge their own fees on top of network fees. Some exchanges, like Binance, are known for having lower fees, while others like Coinbase may charge more, particularly for credit card transactions or withdrawals.

Pro Tip*: If possible, try to make trades during off-peak hours when network congestion is lower. This can help you save on network fees, especially with popular coins like Ethereum.*

Best Practices for Your First Crypto Purchase

To make sure your first crypto purchase goes as smoothly as possible, follow these best practices:

1. **Start Small**: It's tempting to go all-in when making your first purchase, but it's always smart to start with a small amount. This will give you time to get comfortable with the process and minimize risk while you're learning.

2. **Double-Check Your Details**: Always double-check the details before completing any transaction. Ensure that your wallet address is correct, the amount is accurate, and you've reviewed any applicable fees.

3. **Store Your Crypto Safely**: After making your purchase, don't leave your funds on the exchange.

Move them to a secure wallet (see Chapter Four for more on wallet options and security).

4. **Stay Informed**: The crypto market is volatile, and prices can change rapidly. Stay informed about the market conditions and news surrounding your chosen cryptocurrency.

With your exchange account set up and your wallet ready, you're now prepared to make your first cryptocurrency purchase. Whether you start with Bitcoin, Ethereum, or another coin, the key is to take it slow and ensure you're following best practices.

Popular Cryptocurrencies for Beginners

When choosing your first cryptocurrency, it's a good idea to start with the most widely recognized and established coins. Let's explore some of the top cryptocurrencies that beginners could consider.

Bitcoin (BTC)

Bitcoin is the first and most well-known cryptocurrency, often called "digital gold." It was created in 2009 by an anonymous person or group of people under the pseudonym Satoshi Nakamoto. Bitcoin was designed to act as a decentralized currency that operates independently of any government or financial institution. It has since evolved into the most popular cryptocurrency, widely accepted across the globe. Bitcoin's appeal lies in its scarcity (only 21 million BTC will ever be created), its security, and its position as the pioneer of the crypto world.

Why You Should Consider BTC:

- Established and trusted by millions.
- Widely accepted and available on nearly every exchange.
- Seen as a store of value, much like gold.

Ethereum (ETH)

Ethereum is much more than just a digital currency — it's a decentralized platform that enables developers to build and run applications without interference from third parties. Ethereum introduced the concept of smart contracts, which are self-executing contracts with the terms of the agreement directly written into code. This innovation opened up a world of decentralized applications (dApps) and decentralized finance (DeFi), making Ethereum a significant player in the crypto space.

Why You Should Consider ETH:

- Beyond just a currency, it powers an entire ecosystem of decentralized applications.
- Strong developer community and continuous innovation.

- Second largest cryptocurrency by market cap after Bitcoin.

Stablecoins (USDT/USDC)

Stablecoins are a category of cryptocurrencies designed to minimize price volatility. They are often pegged to a stable asset, such as the U.S. dollar. The two most popular stablecoins are Tether (USDT) and USD Coin (USDC), both of which are tied to the value of the U.S. dollar at a 1:1 ratio. Stablecoins are a great option for those who want to participate in the crypto market but are concerned about volatility. They provide stability while allowing you to move in and out of different cryptocurrencies more easily.

Why You Should Consider Stablecoins:

- Provide a stable store of value in a volatile market.
- Useful for trading and as a bridge between traditional fiat and cryptocurrencies.
- Commonly used on exchanges for transferring value quickly and cheaply.

How to Evaluate a Coin/Token

Before you jump into buying any cryptocurrency, it's important to evaluate it carefully to avoid potential pitfalls. Not all cryptocurrencies are created equal, and some are far riskier than others. Here's how to evaluate a coin or token to ensure you are make an informed decision:

1. **Use Case**: A strong use case is the foundation of any successful cryptocurrency. Ask yourself: What problem does this cryptocurrency solve? For example, Bitcoin's use case is as a decentralized currency and store of value, while Ethereum's use case is as a platform for decentralized applications and smart contracts. A cryptocurrency with a clear, real-world application is more likely to succeed in the long term.

    - *Pro Tip: Avoid coins that don't have a clear purpose or seem like they exist purely for speculative trading.*

2. **Development Team**: A cryptocurrency is only as strong as the team behind it. Look for a transparent and reputable team with a track record of success in blockchain or related industries. The team's background can give you insights into how well they can execute their vision. Projects with anonymous or unproven teams can be riskier and should be approached with caution.

    - *Red Flag: If the team lacks experience or doesn't share information openly, that could be a warning sign.*

3. **Partnerships**: Strong partnerships can provide credibility and open up opportunities for adoption. When a cryptocurrency project partners with well-known companies or other projects, it demonstrates that there's interest in what they're building. Partnerships with established organizations also bring a level of trust to the project.

    - *Pro Tip: Check if the project has partnerships with other blockchain platforms, financial institutions, or tech companies. These partnerships can indicate that the project has long-term po-*

tential.

4. **Community and Adoption**: A vibrant and engaged community can make a significant difference in a cryptocurrency's success. Communities drive adoption, create awareness, and can help the project grow through support and development contributions. Look at the size and activity of the community on platforms like Reddit, Twitter, or Discord. A large, active community is often a positive indicator of the project's longevity.
   - *Pro Tip: Beware of projects that rely solely on hype from influencers or marketing. Look for organic community growth and engagement.*

5. **Technology and Innovation**: Finally, assess the technology behind the cryptocurrency. Does it bring something new to the table, or is it simply a copy of another existing project? Innovation can set a project apart from others, making it more likely to attract long-term interest from developers, investors, and users.
   - **Example**: Ethereum's innovation of smart

contracts set it apart from Bitcoin and has driven its growth as the second-largest cryptocurrency by market cap.

Making an Informed Decision

By now, you should feel more confident about choosing which cryptocurrency to buy first. Whether you go with established options like Bitcoin and Ethereum or opt for stablecoins like USDT for stability, the key is to start with what you understand. And *always, always* do your research before jumping into any coin or token. Evaluating a project's use case, team, partnerships, and community can help you make informed decisions and avoid the more speculative or riskier investments.

Next, we'll move into the crucial topic of securing your crypto with wallets. You've bought your first crypto—now let's make sure it's stored safely!

Chapter Four

Understanding Crypto Wallets

YOUR KEYS, YOUR COINS. You wouldn't keep all your cash under your mattress, would you? The same logic applies to cryptocurrency. Once you've bought your first coins, the next big question is: where do you store them? That's where crypto wallets come in. Think of a crypto wallet as your digital safe—except, instead of storing physical cash, it stores your access to your digital assets.

In this chapter, we'll cover the types of wallets available, how to set them up, and most importantly, how to keep your crypto safe. By the end, you'll have a firm grasp on how to manage your digital assets securely.

Hot vs. Cold Wallets

There are two primary types of crypto wallets: hot wallets and cold wallets. Each type has its own pros and cons, and the best choice for you will depend on how you plan to use your crypto.

Hot Wallets (Software Wallets)

Hot wallets are connected to the internet and are generally used for everyday transactions. They're fast, convenient, and easy to set up, making them a popular choice for beginners. Most exchanges, like Binance and Coinbase, offer built-in hot wallets, allowing you to store your crypto directly on their platforms.

Pros:

- Easy to set up and use.
- Ideal for small, frequent transactions.
- Accessible from anywhere with an internet connection.

Cons:

- More vulnerable to hacking and theft since

they're always connected to the internet.

- If the platform hosting your wallet gets hacked, you could lose your funds.

Cold Wallets (Hardware and Paper Wallets)

Cold wallets, on the other hand, are offline and not connected to the internet. They're considered the safest way to store large amounts of crypto because they're immune to online hacks. The most common types of cold wallets are hardware wallets (like the Ledger or Trezor) and paper wallets (which involve printing your private keys on paper and storing them securely).

Pros:

- Extremely secure since they're offline and protected from online threats.
- Ideal for long-term storage of large amounts of crypto.

Cons:

- Less convenient for everyday transactions.
- If you lose access to the physical wallet (like losing your hardware wallet or damaging your paper

wallet), you could lose your crypto.

Pros and Cons of Different Wallets

When it comes to choosing the right wallet, you'll also need to decide between different platforms. Here's a breakdown of the most common wallet types and how they work:

1. **Desktop Wallets**: These are installed on your computer and give you full control over your private keys. Popular desktop wallets include Exodus and Electrum. They're more secure than web wallets, but if your computer is compromised, so is your wallet.

2. **Mobile Wallets**: These are apps installed on your Smartphone. Mobile wallets like Trust Wallet and MetaMask allow you to send and receive crypto on the go. They're great for day-to-day use but come with security risks, especially if your phone is lost or hacked.

3. **Web Wallets**: Web wallets are accessed through your browser and are often tied to exchanges (like the wallets offered by Binance or Coinbase). While they're easy to access and use, they're the least secure option since they're hosted by a third party.

4. **Paper Wallets**: Paper wallets are a form of cold storage where your public and private keys are printed on paper. It's an offline method and immune to hacking, but if the paper is lost or damaged, your crypto is gone forever.

How to Set Up and Secure Your Wallet

Now that you understand the different types of wallets, let's walk through the process of setting one up. We'll use a popular mobile wallet, Trust Wallet, as an example. Trust Wallet is a beginner-friendly mobile app that supports a wide range of cryptocurrencies and is known for its ease of use.

Step-by-Step Guide to Setting Up a Mobile Wallet:

1. **Download the App**: Head to the App Store or Google Play and download Trust Wallet.

2. **Create a New Wallet**: Open the app and tap "Create a New Wallet." You'll be prompted to agree to the terms and conditions.

3. **Backup Your Seed Phrase**: This is the most important step. The app will provide you with a 12-word recovery phrase (also known as a seed phrase). Write this down on paper and store it somewhere safe—don't take a screenshot or store it online. If you lose your phone or need to recover your wallet, this seed phrase is the only way to regain access to your funds.

    - ***Pro Tip***: *Never share your seed phrase with anyone. Anyone with access to your seed phrase has complete control over your wallet.*

4. **Confirm Your Seed Phrase**: Trust Wallet will ask you to confirm your seed phrase by selecting the words in the correct order. This ensures that you've backed it up correctly.

5. **Set Up Security**: Enable security features like biometric login (fingerprint or face recognition) or a PIN code for added protection. You should also enable two-factor authentication (2FA) if the wallet supports it.

6. **Start Using Your Wallet**: Once everything is set up, you can start receiving, storing, and sending crypto. Simply tap the "Receive" button to view your wallet address and share it with others to receive funds.

Transferring Funds from Exchange to Wallet

Once you've set up your wallet, the next step is to transfer your crypto from the exchange where you purchased it (e.g., Binance, Coinbase) to your personal wallet for safekeeping. Here's how:

1. **Log into Your Exchange Account**: Go to the exchange where you purchased your crypto and log into your account.

2. **Select Withdraw**: Navigate to the "Withdraw" section of the exchange. Here, you'll be asked to enter the amount of crypto you want to transfer and the wallet address where it's going.

3. **Copy Your Wallet Address**: Open your Trust Wallet app (or whichever wallet you've set up) and find your receive address. Copy this address and paste it into the withdrawal section on your exchange account.

   - ***Pro Tip**: Always double-check the wallet address before sending. Sending crypto to the wrong address can't be undone, and you may lose your funds.*

4. **Confirm the Transaction**: Once you've entered the amount and the correct wallet address, confirm the transaction. Depending on the cryptocurrency, it may take anywhere from a few minutes to a few hours for the funds to appear in your wallet.

5. **Verify the Transfer**: Open your wallet and verify that the funds have been received. You'll be able

to see the amount and transaction details in your wallet's transaction history.

Best Ways to Secure Your Private Keys

Your private key is the most critical piece of information associated with your wallet. It's what gives you access to your crypto, and losing it means losing your funds. Here are some best practices for securing your private keys:

1. **Keep Your Keys Offline**: Never store your private keys on an online service (e.g., cloud storage or email). This makes them vulnerable to hacking. Instead, use offline methods like cold storage or a hardware wallet.

2. **Use a Hardware Wallet for Large Holdings**: If you're holding a significant amount of crypto, consider investing in a hardware wallet like Ledger or Trezor. These devices store your private keys offline, offering a higher level of security than software wallets.

3. **Don't Share Your Keys**: This might seem obvious, but it's worth repeating: never share your private keys or recovery phrases with anyone. No legitimate service or individual will ever ask for this information.

4. **Enable 2FA**: If your wallet or exchange offers two-factor authentication, enable it. This adds an extra layer of security, making it harder for unauthorized users to access your account.

5. **Keep Backup Copies**: Make multiple physical copies of your seed phrase and store them in different, secure locations. This ensures you have a backup in case one copy is lost or destroyed.

By now, you should have a solid understanding of how crypto wallets work and why they are essential to secure your digital assets. Whether you choose a hot wallet for everyday transactions or a cold wallet for long-term storage, remember that the security of your funds is in your hands. Always follow best practices when setting up and using your wallet, and never underestimate the importance of keeping your private keys safe.

Next, we'll dive into the exciting world of crypto trading. But before that, take a moment to pat yourself on the back—you've already mastered one of the most important steps in your crypto journey!

Chapter Five

Intro to Trading: Key Concepts and Tools

So, you've bought your first cryptocurrency — congratulations! Now, you might be wondering what comes next. If you're looking to dive deeper into the world of crypto, trading is an exciting avenue that allows you to profit from the market's ups and downs. But before you jump in, it's crucial to understand the key concepts and tools that traders rely on to make informed decisions.

In this chapter, we'll provide an overview of essential trading concepts, including how to read price charts, basic technical analysis, and the different trading strategies used by crypto traders. While we won't be diving too deep into advanced trading tactics, this chapter will give you a solid foundation to get started in the world of trading.

Price Charts and Candlesticks

One of the first things you'll encounter in crypto trading is price charts. These charts display the price movements of a cryptocurrency over time and are the foundation of any trading strategy. While they might look complex at first, once you understand the basics, they become an invaluable tool for making trading decisions.

A popular way to represent price data is through candlestick charts. Unlike simple line charts, candlestick charts provide more detailed information about price movements within a specific time period.

Basics of Candlestick Charts

Candlesticks represent the price action of a cryptocurrency over a given time frame (such as one hour, one day, or one week). Each candlestick shows four key pieces of information:

1. **Open**: The price of the cryptocurrency at the beginning of the time period.

2. **Close**: The price of the cryptocurrency at the end of the time period.

3. **High**: The highest price the cryptocurrency reached during the time period.

4. **Low**: The lowest price the cryptocurrency dropped to during the time period.

Candlesticks also have bodies and wicks:

- The **body** of the candlestick represents the range between the opening and closing prices. A green or white body indicates that the price closed higher than it opened (bullish), while a red or black body indicates that the price closed lower than it opened (bearish).

- The **wicks** (also known as shadows) extend from the body to show the high and low prices during the time period.

By analyzing candlestick patterns, traders can get insights into market sentiment and potential future price movements.

Support and Resistance Levels

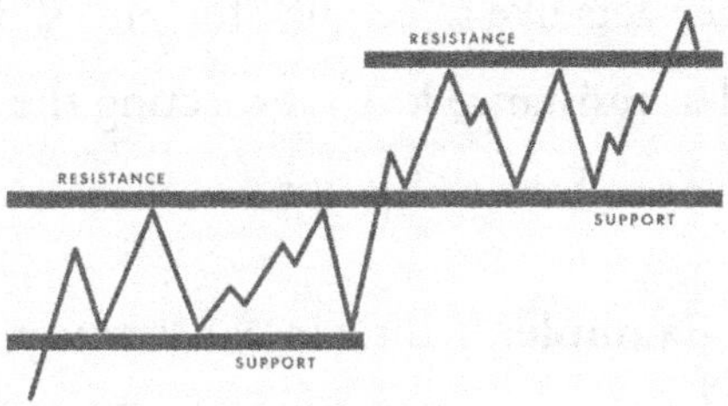

Two key concepts in trading are support and resistance levels, which help traders identify potential points where the price may stop and reverse direction.

1. **Support**: This is a price level where a cryptocurrency finds buying pressure and stops falling. Support levels act like a "floor" for prices, helping to prevent them from dropping further. Traders often buy at support levels, expecting the price to bounce back up.

   ◦ **Example**: If Bitcoin consistently bounces

back up every time it reaches $60,000, then $60,000 is considered a support level.

2. **Resistance**: Resistance is the opposite of support. It's a price level where a cryptocurrency faces selling pressure and struggles to rise above. Resistance acts like a "ceiling" for prices. Traders may sell at resistance levels, expecting the price to fall after reaching this point.
    - **Example**: If Bitcoin consistently struggles to break above $64,000, then $64,000 is considered a resistance level.

Why Do These Levels Matter?

- **Support and resistance** levels help traders make decisions on where to enter or exit a trade. By understanding these levels, traders can anticipate potential reversals and set more effective stop-loss and take-profit orders.

Technical Analysis vs. Fundamental Analysis

When it comes to analyzing the crypto market, there are two main approaches: technical analysis and fundamental analysis. Both methods have their own strengths, and many traders use a combination of the two to inform their strategies.

1. **Technical Analysis**: Technical analysis focuses on past price data, volume, and patterns to predict future price movements. It is based on the belief that market trends tend to repeat themselves, and by studying charts and technical indicators, traders can identify opportunities for profit.

    - **Tools for Technical Analysis** (more on this below) include candlestick charts, moving averages, and momentum indicators like the Relative Strength Index (RSI).

    - **Best for**: Short-term traders who rely on price trends and patterns to make decisions.

2. **Fundamental Analysis**: Fundamental analysis looks at the intrinsic value of a cryptocurrency by analyzing its underlying technology, team, market potential, and real-world use cases. Instead of focusing on price charts, fundamental analysts look at factors such as the development team, partnerships, and adoption rates to evaluate a cryptocurrency's long-term potential.

    - **Tools for Analysis:** Indicators, Moving Averages, RSI, Moving Average Convergence Divergence (MACD).

    - **Best for**: Long-term investors who are more interested in a cryptocurrency's overall growth and potential rather than short-term price movements.

To get deeper insights into the market, traders use technical indicators that provide data beyond what you can see on price charts alone. Here are a few key indicators that can help you understand market trends and momentum:

1. **Moving Averages**: Moving averages smooth out price data over a set period of time to help traders identify trends. The Simple Moving Av-

erage (SMA) calculates the average price over a specific time period (e.g., 20 days, 50 days, etc.). If the current price is above the moving average, it can signal an uptrend, while prices below the moving average may signal a downtrend.

2. **Relative Strength Index (RSI)**: RSI is a momentum indicator that measures the speed and change of price movements. It ranges from 0 to 100, with levels above 70 indicating that the asset may be overbought (suggesting a price correction is likely), and levels below 30 indicating that it may be oversold (suggesting a potential price increase).

3. **Moving Average Convergence Divergence (MACD)**: MACD is another momentum indicator that shows the relationship between two moving averages (a short-term and a long-term one). When the MACD line crosses above the signal line, it can indicate a bullish trend, and when it crosses below, it can signal a bearish trend.

Why These Tools Matter: Indicators help traders make sense of price trends and momentum, allowing them to spot potential buying and selling opportunities. They provide valuable insights into the health and direction of the market.

The News and Its Impact on Crypto Prices

In the world of crypto, news and announcements can have a dramatic impact on prices. From regulatory decisions to major corporate investments, the market often reacts strongly to news information.

1. **Positive News**: Positive developments, such as a major company accepting Bitcoin as payment or a government providing favorable regulations can cause prices to spike. For example, when Tesla announced it had bought $1.5 billion worth of Bitcoin in 2021, the price surged significantly.

2. **Negative News**: On the flip side, negative news, such as regulatory crackdowns or high-profile exchange hacks, can send prices plummeting. For instance, China's repeated bans on cryptocurrency trading and mining have caused several market

downturns over the years.

Pro Tip: *Staying informed and monitoring the news regularly can help you anticipate price movements and adjust your trading strategy accordingly.*

Day Trading vs. Swing Trading vs. HODLing

When trading crypto, there are different strategies you can choose based on your time commitment, risk tolerance, and goals. Let's explore three of the most common types of traders:

1. **Day Traders**: Day traders buy and sell cryptocurrencies within the same day, sometimes making multiple trades over the course of a few hours. This strategy relies on small price movements and requires constant attention to the market. Day traders often use technical analysis to make quick decisions and capitalize on short-term price fluctuations.

    - **Pros**: Potential for quick profits.

   - **Cons**: Requires a lot of time, focus, and a deep understanding of market trends.

2. **Swing Traders**: Swing traders look for opportunities where they can hold a position for days or weeks, aiming to profit from price "swings." They don't monitor the market as closely as day traders but rely on both technical and fundamental analysis to identify medium-term trends.

   - **Pros**: Less time-intensive than day trading.
   - **Cons**: Requires patience and the ability to ride out market fluctuations.

3. **HODLers**: HODL (Hold On for Dear Life) is a popular strategy among long-term investors who buy and hold cryptocurrency for an extended period, often ignoring short-term price volatility. HODLers believe in the long-term potential of cryptocurrencies and are not concerned with daily price movements.

   - **Pros**: Requires little daily maintenance, long-term growth potential.

- **Cons**: May miss out on short-term profit opportunities.

Setting the Stage for Your Trading Journey

By now, you have a solid understanding of the key concepts and tools used by crypto traders. Whether you're looking at price charts, analyzing indicators like RSI, or keeping an eye on the news, these tools will help you make more informed decisions.

As you explore the different types of traders—whether you lean towards day trading, swing trading or HODLing—remember that each strategy comes with its own set of pros and cons. The most important thing is to choose a trading style that fits your goals, risk tolerance, and time commitment.

In the next chapter, we'll dive into risk management and crypto strategies, essential topics that will help you protect your investments and minimize potential losses.

Chapter Six

Risk Management and Crypto Strategies

ALWAYS PLAY IT SMART by protecting your investments. When it comes to cryptocurrency, the potential for high rewards is real — but so are the risks; this is true every time. Crypto markets can be incredibly volatile, and without a solid risk management plan, even seasoned traders can suffer major losses. This chapter focuses on the strategies that will help you protect your capital and make smart decisions that balance risk and reward.

We'll cover the importance of diversification, how to use stop-loss and take-profit orders, and explain how strategies like dollar-cost averaging (DCA) can reduce risk. Finally, we'll explore the emotional side of trading and how to keep a cool head in the often chaotic world of crypto.

Crypto Diversification

One important lesson to bear in mind is to learn to never "put all your eggs in one basket."

One of the first lessons in risk management is diversification. In simple terms, this means not putting all your money into one investment. Instead, spread it across multiple assets to minimize your exposure to any single cryptocurrency's volatility. The goal is to protect your portfolio from sharp declines in any one asset, especially in a market as unpredictable as crypto.

Why Diversification Matters

While Bitcoin may be the most popular cryptocurrency, the crypto market is filled with thousands of altcoins, each with different levels of risk and reward. Diversifying your portfolio across multiple coins can help you take advantage of growth opportunities while also protecting your capital from the wild price swings often seen in individual cryptocurrencies.

How to Diversify Your Portfolio

- **Invest in Multiple Cryptos**: Instead of putting all your money into Bitcoin, consider spreading your investment across several coins, such as Ethereum, stablecoins like USDT, and a few other carefully selected altcoins with long-term potential.

- **Balance High-Risk, High-Reward with Stability**: While it's tempting to go all-in on high-potential, high-risk coins, it is important to balance them with more stable investments such as Bitcoin or stablecoins, which tend to be less volatile. A diversified portfolio will help to ensure that when one part of the market dips, the other might still be performing well.

Don't Put All Your Money in One Coin

Cryptocurrencies are known for their unpredictability. Even the most solid projects can experience sudden crashes due to market sentiment, regulatory news, or security concerns. Putting all your capital into one coin means that if that coin plummets, you could lose a significant portion—or all—of your investment.

Example: Imagine you put all your money into an altcoin that looked promising due to its rapid price growth. Suddenly, news breaks that the development team is abandoning the project, or there's a major security flaw. In an instant, the value of the coin could drop dramatically, leaving you with massive losses. If you had diversified across several coins, only a fraction of your portfolio would be affected by this single event.

How to Create a Balance

As a crypto investor, it's essential to balance high-risk, high-reward assets with more stable options to reduce the overall risk in your portfolio.

1. **High-Risk, High-Reward Assets**: These are often smaller, lesser-known altcoins that have the potential for massive gains—but also carry the risk of huge losses. Investing in these coins can be profitable, but it should be done cautiously and in smaller amounts.

    - **Example**: Altcoins like Solana or Avalanche may show huge price jumps over a short period, but they can also be highly volatile.

2. **Stablecoins**: Stablecoins like USDT or USDC are pegged to a stable asset, such as the U.S. dollar, making them less volatile than other cryptocurrencies. While they don't offer the same high returns as riskier coins, they provide a safe haven for your capital during market downturns.

3. **Blue-Chip Cryptos**: Bitcoin and Ethereum are often considered "blue-chip" cryptocurrencies due to their dominance and long-standing positions in the market. While they still experience volatility, they're generally viewed as more stable than newer, lesser-known coins.

Pro Tip*: Aim to balance your portfolio by investing a portion of your funds in high-risk, high-reward altcoins while keeping the majority in blue-chip cryptos and stablecoins. This balance allows you to capture potential gains while minimizing the risk of major losses.*

Stop-Loss and Take-Profit Orders

One of the most critical aspects of risk management is knowing when to cut your losses or lock in your profits. That's where stop-loss and take-profit orders come into play. These tools help you automate your trades, protecting your capital when prices fall and securing your gains when prices rise.

1. **Stop-Loss Orders**: A stop-loss order is a pre-set

order that automatically sells your crypto when it reaches a certain price, preventing further losses. For example, if you bought Bitcoin at $30,000, you could set a stop-loss at $28,000. If the price drops to that level, your Bitcoin will automatically be sold, protecting you from further declines.

- **Why It Is Important**:
    - Stop-loss orders remove the emotional aspect of trading. Instead of panic selling when prices dip, your stop-loss automatically sells for you at the pre-set level.
    - It helps preserve your capital, allowing you to re-enter the market at a better time.

2. **Take-Profit Orders**: A take-profit order is the opposite of a stop-loss. It automatically sells your crypto when it reaches a certain profit level. For example, if you bought Bitcoin at $30,000 and set a take-profit at $35,000, the order would trigger when Bitcoin's price hits that target, locking in your profits.

- **Why It Is Important**:
  - Take-profit orders help ensure you don't miss out on gains by waiting too long to sell.
  - This is a great way to secure profits when you can't monitor the market 24/7.

Pro Tip: *It's a good idea to use stop-loss and take-profit orders together. This way, you can protect yourself from both sudden drops and the risk of holding on too long and missing the chance to lock in gains.*

Reducing Risk over Time

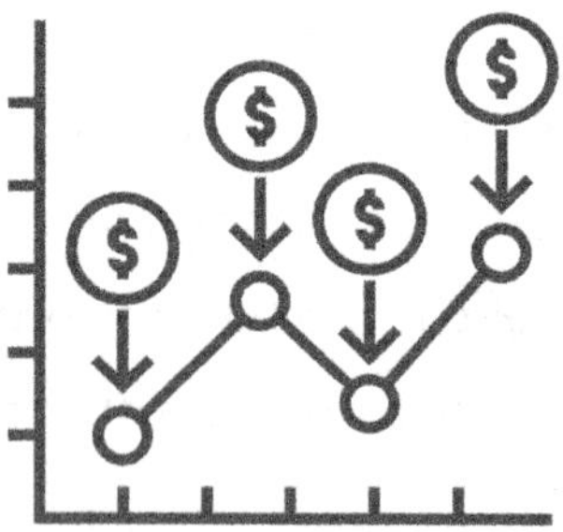

One of the most popular and effective risk management strategies in crypto is **dollar-cost averaging (DCA)**. This strategy involves investing a fixed amount of money at regular intervals (e.g., weekly or monthly), regardless of the asset's price. Over time, this helps smooth out the effects of market volatility.

Why DCA Works: Instead of trying to time the market—an approach that even professional traders struggle with—DCA allows you to gradually build your position in a cryptocurrency over time. By buying in both high and low markets, you reduce the risk of buying at an inflated price.

Example: Let's say you want to invest $1,200 in Bitcoin over the course of a year. Instead of investing the full $1,200 at once, you could invest $100 per month. This way, you buy more Bitcoin when prices are low and less when prices are high, averaging out your purchase price over time.

The Impact of Emotions on Trading Decisions

In the volatile world of crypto, emotions can often lead to poor decision-making. Fear, greed, and impatience are the enemies of disciplined investing. Successful traders and investors know how to manage their emotions and stick to their strategy, even when the market feels chaotic.

1. **Fear of Missing Out (FOMO)**: When prices are rising rapidly, it's easy to feel like you're missing out on huge gains. This often leads to buying at the peak of a rally, only to see prices crash soon after. The key is to avoid FOMO and stick to your strategy instead of chasing the hype.

2. **Fear, Uncertainty, and Doubt (FUD)**: The opposite of FOMO, FUD occurs when negative news or rumors cause you to panic and sell off your holdings. While it's important to stay informed, it's also crucial to filter out market noise and avoid panic-selling during temporary market dips.

3. **Greed**: When the market is bullish, it's tempting to hold onto your assets for too long, hoping for even greater profits. But greed can lead to missing the chance to lock in gains, especially if the market reverses unexpectedly.

The Importance of a Disciplined Trading Mindset

The best traders and investors maintain discipline by sticking to their strategies, regardless of market fluctuations. Here's how to develop a disciplined mindset when trading:

- **Have a Plan**: Set clear goals for each trade, including your entry and exit points. Know how much you're willing to risk and when you'll take profits.

- **Use Stop-Loss and Take-Profit Orders**: As mentioned earlier, these automated tools help you stick to your plan and remove emotions from the equation.

- **Stay Patient**: Crypto markets are volatile, and prices can fluctuate dramatically in a short time. Successful traders remain patient and avoid making impulsive decisions based on short-term price movements.

Wise risk management is the key to long-term success in cryptocurrency. Whether you're a seasoned trader or just starting out, using strategies such as diversification, dollar-cost averaging, and stop-loss orders will help protect your capital and grow your investments over time. And perhaps most importantly, maintaining a disciplined mindset will allow you to navigate the ups and downs of the crypto market without letting emotions get in the way.

In the next chapter, we'll dive into how to store and track your investments, ensuring your hard-earned crypto remains safe and secure.

Chapter Seven

Storing and Tracking Your Investments

In a market as fast-moving as cryptocurrency, keeping tabs on your portfolio and maintaining detailed records of your trades can make all the difference when it comes to managing your assets effectively.

In this chapter, we'll explore how to track your portfolio's performance using popular tools, the importance of keeping detailed records, and what you need to know about the tax implications of your crypto investments.

Portfolio Trackers

One of the key challenges in cryptocurrency investing is keeping track of the value and performance of your investments, especially if you hold multiple coins across different exchanges and wallets. That's where portfolio trackers come in handy.

A portfolio tracker allows you to monitor the current value of all your crypto holdings in real-time. You can link your exchange accounts and wallets to the tracker, making it easy to see how much your portfolio is worth, how it's performing, and how your investments are allocated.

Benefits of Using a Portfolio Tracker:

- **Centralized Overview**: If you have investments spread across different platforms, a portfolio tracker provides a single, centralized view of your entire portfolio.

- **Real-Time Updates**: Track your portfolio's performance in real-time as the crypto market moves. Many trackers allow you to set up price alerts, so you're notified of significant price changes.

- **Performance Metrics**: These tools often offer performance metrics, showing you the percentage increase or decrease of your portfolio and individual assets over specific time frames.

Tools to Track Portfolio Performance

Two of the most popular portfolio trackers for crypto investors are CoinGecko and CoinMarketCap. Let's take a closer look at how these platforms can help you stay on top of your investments:

CoinGecko

CoinGecko is one of the most widely used platforms for tracking cryptocurrency prices and portfolio performance. It provides real-time data on thousands of cryptocurrencies and offers portfolio tracking features where you can input your holdings and monitor them in one place. CoinGecko also offers historical price data, so you can see how your investments have performed over time.

- **Key Features**:

- Price alerts and notifications.
- Historical charts to monitor trends.
- Access to over 6,000 cryptocurrencies and 400+ exchanges.

CoinMarketCap

CoinMarketCap is another powerful tool that tracks cryptocurrency prices and helps you manage your portfolio. Like CoinGecko, it offers real-time price updates, historical data, and portfolio tracking. It also provides market insights, including circulating supply, volume, and market capitalization for each cryptocurrency.

- **Key Features**:
  - In-depth market analysis, including price volatility and trading volumes.
  - Real-time tracking of over 10,000 cryptocurrencies.
  - Integration with multiple exchanges for easy portfolio management.

How to Use These Tools:

- **Manual Entry**: If you prefer not to link your accounts, you can manually enter the amounts of each cryptocurrency you own and track them over time.
- **Exchange Integration**: Both platforms allow you to connect your exchange accounts. This automatically updates your portfolio based on your latest trades and holdings.

Tax Implications of Crypto Investments

One of the most important, yet often overlooked, aspects of cryptocurrency investing is to understand the tax implications. In many countries, cryptocurrency transactions are subject to taxes, and failing to properly report your crypto gains can lead to significant penalties. Let's break down how taxes typically work in crypto and why it's critical to stay compliant.

How Crypto Taxes Work

In most jurisdictions, cryptocurrencies are treated as assets or property, which means that any time you buy, sell, or trade crypto, it's considered a taxable event. The tax you owe depends on whether you've made a profit or incurred a loss when you sell or trade the asset.

- **Capital Gains Tax**: If you sell cryptocurrency for more than you paid for it, you're subject to capital gains tax on the profit. The rate depends on how long you held the asset—short-term capital gains (usually less than a year) are taxed at a higher rate than long-term capital gains (more than a year).

- **Capital Losses**: If you sell cryptocurrency for less than you bought it, you can claim a capital loss, which may offset other capital gains and reduce your tax liability.

- **Crypto-to-Crypto Trades**: Many investors are unaware that trading one cryptocurrency for another (for example, trading Bitcoin for Ethereum) is also a taxable event in many countries, and any gains made in the trade need to be reported.

***Pro Tip**: Many portfolio trackers, like CoinGecko and CoinMarketCap, allow you to export your transaction data for tax reporting purposes, making the process much easier.*

Tax Software for Crypto

There are also dedicated crypto tax software platforms like CoinTracker and Koinly, that automatically track your transactions and calculate your capital gains or losses. These tools can integrate with your portfolio tracker or exchange accounts to pull in your data, generate tax reports, and help ensure compliance with tax authorities.

Why Keep Detailed Records of Your Trades

Keeping detailed records of your trades isn't just for tax purposes — it's also a crucial part of managing your portfolio effectively. Here's why:

1. **Track Your Performance**: By keeping records

of each trade, you can analyze how well your strategy is working. Are you making more profitable trades than losing trades? Which coins are performing better over time? Without proper records, it's difficult to assess your success and adjust your strategy.

2. **Audit and Reporting Requirements**: Depending on your country's tax laws, you may be required to produce records of your crypto transactions for tax audits. Having clear and organized records ensures you will be prepared to provide this information if needed.

3. **Reduce Errors**: With so many transactions happening in the fast-paced crypto market, it's easy to lose track of your trades. Detailed records help you stay organized and avoid errors when calculating your gains, losses, and tax liability.

What to Include in Your Records:

- **Date and time** of the transaction.
- **Amount** of cryptocurrency involved.

- **Price** in your local currency at the time of the transaction.
- **Transaction fees** (if any).
- **Exchange platform** where the transaction took place.

Tracking your portfolio and keeping detailed records are essential parts of successful cryptocurrency investing. Tools like CoinGecko and CoinMarketCap make it easy to monitor your investments and keep an eye on the market in real-time. By understanding the tax implications and staying organized with your trades, you'll ensure that your crypto journey is both profitable and compliant.

Next, we'll explore how to avoid common pitfalls and scams in the crypto world, arming you with the knowledge you need to stay safe while navigating this exciting space.

Chapter Eight

Avoiding Common Pitfalls and Scams

THE CRYPTO WORLD OFFERS exciting opportunities, but it also comes with risks, especially for newcomers. Scams, fraud, and risky schemes are all too common, and without the proper knowledge, even experienced investors can fall victim. In this chapter, we'll explore how to protect yourself from common pitfalls like pump-and-dump schemes, fraudulent projects, and phishing attacks. By the end, you'll have the tools to navigate the crypto space more safely and confidently.

Pump-and-Dump Schemes

One of the most notorious scams in the cryptocurrency world is the pump-and-dump scheme. This type of scam often takes advantage of inexperienced traders and the volatility of smaller altcoins.

A pump-and-dump scheme is a type of market manipulation where a group of people artificially inflate the price of a cryptocurrency (the pump) by spreading misleading information or generating hype. Once the price has risen significantly, the group behind the scheme sells off their holdings (the dump), leaving unsuspecting investors with worthless coins as the price crashes back down.

These schemes often target lesser-known cryptocurrencies with low liquidity because it's easier to manipulate their prices. Social media platforms, especially Telegram groups or Discord channels, are commonly used to organize pump-and-dump schemes.

Example: In 2021, several small cryptocurrencies saw rapid, unsustainable price increases due to coordinated pump-and-dump efforts, leading to major losses for those who bought into the hype at the peak.

How to Recognize a Pump-and-Dump Scheme

- **Unexplained Rapid Price Increases**: If you notice a cryptocurrency suddenly skyrocketing in price without any significant news or development backing the rise, it could be a pump-and-dump scheme.
- **Hype on Social Media**: Be wary of unknown coins being aggressively promoted on social media or in online communities. Pump-and-dump organizers often use these channels to create excitement and lure in inexperienced traders.
- **Low Liquidity**: Pump-and-dump schemes typically target low-liquidity coins that are easier to manipulate. Always check the coin's trading volume before investing.

***Pro Tip**: If something seems too good to be true, it probably is. Avoid jumping on the hype train for obscure coins and do your research before making any investment.*

Recognizing Fraudulent Projects

As exciting as Initial Coin Offerings (ICOs) and Decentralized Finance (DeFi) projects can be, they are also prime targets for fraudsters. Many investors have lost money by investing in fraudulent projects that never deliver on their promises. Here's how to spot the red flags.

1. **What Is an ICO?** An **Initial Coin Offering (ICO)** is a way for cryptocurrency projects to raise capital by selling their tokens to early investors. While ICOs were once a popular way to invest in new projects, they've become a breeding ground for scams, especially since regulations around ICOs are often lax or non-existent.

2. **What Is DeFi? Decentralized Finance (DeFi)** refers to blockchain-based financial services that don't rely on traditional intermediaries like

banks. DeFi platforms offer services like lending, borrowing, and trading, all through decentralized protocols. While DeFi has great potential, it's also rife with poorly designed projects and scams.

Red Flags in ICOs and DeFi Projects

- **Lack of Transparency**: If the team behind the project is anonymous or provides little information about their backgrounds, that's a major red flag. Legitimate projects are usually led by teams with verifiable credentials.
- **Unrealistic Promises**: If a project promises guaranteed returns or claims it will disrupt an entire industry without clear proof, be skeptical. Scammers often use exaggerated claims to lure in investors.
- **No Working Product**: Many fraudulent ICOs launch without a working product or a clear

roadmap for development. If the project doesn't have a demo, prototype or at least a clear vision of how it will execute its plan, avoid it.

- **Lack of Code Audits**: In DeFi, smart contracts are the backbone of the system. Legitimate DeFi projects undergo independent smart contract audits to ensure their code is secure and doesn't have vulnerabilities. If a DeFi project doesn't have an audit, proceed with caution.

Pro Tip: *Before investing in any ICO or DeFi project, check platforms like ICOBench or DeFiPulse for ratings, reviews, and audits to verify the legitimacy of the project.*

More Security Tips

In addition to market scams, cryptocurrency users must be vigilant against phishing attacks and other forms of cyber fraud. Since crypto transactions are irreversible, once your funds are stolen, there's no way to recover them. Here's how to protect yourself from common threats.

1. **Phishing Attacks:** Phishing attacks involve tricking you into revealing sensitive information

like your private keys, passwords, or two-factor authentication codes. Attackers usually do this by posing as a legitimate service—such as your exchange or wallet provider—and asking you to enter your credentials on a fake website or through an email link.

- How to Stay Safe:
    - **Double-Check URLs**: Always verify the website's URL before entering any information. Scammers often create fake websites that look like the real thing but have slight variations in the URL (e.g., "coinba se.com" might be faked as "co1nbase.com ").
    - **Be Wary of Emails**: Never click on links in unsolicited emails or messages that ask for personal information. Legitimate companies will never ask for sensitive details via email.
    - **Enable Two-Factor Authentication (2FA)**: Always enable 2FA on your ex-

change and wallet accounts. Even if a scammer gets your password, they'll need your second authentication method (such as a code from an app like Google Authenticator) to access your account.

2. **Fake Wallets and Exchanges:** Scammers sometimes create fake cryptocurrency wallets or exchanges to trick users into depositing their funds. These fake platforms look legitimate but are designed to steal your crypto once you've transferred it.

    ◦ How to Stay Safe:

        - **Use Trusted Platforms**: Only use well-known, reputable wallets and exchanges that have been around for a while and have strong security measures in place.
        - **Check Reviews**: Before downloading a wallet or signing up for an exchange, check reviews from multiple sources to ensure the platform is legitimate.

3. **SIM Swapping:** In a **SIM swapping attack**, a hacker tricks your mobile phone provider into transferring your phone number to a new SIM card that they control. Once they have your phone number, they can bypass SMS-based two-factor authentication (2FA) and gain access to your accounts.
   - How to Stay Safe:
     - **Use App-Based 2FA**: Instead of relying on SMS-based 2FA, use an authenticator app like Google Authenticator or Authy. These apps provide stronger protection against SIM swapping attacks.
     - **Set a PIN with Your Mobile Provider**: Many mobile providers allow you to set a PIN or password on your account, adding an extra layer of security.

Vigilance Equals Safety

The crypto space is filled with opportunities, but it's also home to various scams and frauds that can trip up even the most cautious investors. By learning how to spot pump-and-dump schemes, avoid fraudulent ICOs and DeFi projects, and protect yourself from phishing attacks and fraud, you'll be well-equipped to navigate the market safely.

In the final chapter, we'll explore some advanced concepts for those curious to delve deeper into the crypto world, including margin trading, DeFi investments, and NFTs.

Chapter Nine

Advanced Concepts for the Curious

By now, you've learned the essentials of cryptocurrency trading and investing. If you're eager to expand your knowledge, this chapter explores advanced concepts that are reshaping the crypto landscape. While these topics may seem complex, they offer new opportunities for those who are willing to dive deeper. We'll discuss margin and leverage trading, the booming world of Decentralized Finance (DeFi), and how NFTs have revolutionized digital ownership.

Margin and Leverage Trading

Margin and leverage trading are strategies that can amplify potential profits—but they also come with significant risks. For beginners, these trading methods should be approached with caution.

1. **What Is Margin Trading?** In margin trading, you borrow funds from the exchange or a broker to increase your trading position. This allows you to trade with more money than you actually have in your account, amplifying your potential gains (or losses).

    - **Example**: If you have $1,000 in your account but use 2:1 margin, you can trade as if you have $2,000. While this can double your profits, it can also double your losses.

2. **What Is Leverage? Leverage** refers to the ratio of borrowed funds to your own. For example, if you use 5x leverage, you're borrowing five times your original capital. Leverage trading magnifies both gains and losses, which is why it's considered

risky, especially in volatile markets like crypto.

Why Beginners Should Be Cautious:

- **Increased Risk**: While margin and leverage trading can generate larger profits, they also expose you to greater losses. In extreme cases, traders can lose more than their initial investment.
- **Liquidation**: If the market moves against your position and your balance drops below a certain level, your position can be liquidated, meaning your assets are sold to cover the loss.

Decentralized Finance Investments

Decentralized Finance (DeFi) is a fast-growing sector of the crypto industry, offering a new way to manage financial services without the need for traditional banks or intermediaries. DeFi platforms operate on blockchain technology, using smart contracts to enable lending, borrowing, and trading- and earning interest on assets.

What Is DeFi?

DeFi platforms are decentralized applications (dApps) that provide financial services such as loans, insurance, savings, and trading. Unlike traditional finance, which relies on centralized institutions, DeFi operates on a blockchain, allowing users to control their assets directly.

How DeFi Is Changing Crypto Trading

- **Accessibility**: DeFi opens financial services to anyone with an internet connection, regardless of location or financial background.
- **Transparency**: All transactions on DeFi platforms are recorded on the blockchain, making them transparent and secure.
- **Yield Opportunities**: DeFi offers various ways to earn passive income, including yield farming and staking (explained below).

New Ways to Earn Rewards

DeFi has introduced new ways for crypto investors to earn rewards beyond simple price appreciation. Two of the most popular methods are yield farming and staking.

- **Yield Farming**: In yield farming, users lend or stake their cryptocurrency in DeFi protocols in exchange for rewards, typically in the form of additional tokens. Yield farming allows you to earn returns on your holdings, but it comes with risks, such as market volatility and smart contract vulnerabilities.

- **Staking**: Staking involves locking up your cryptocurrency in a network to support its operations, such as validating transactions. In return, you earn rewards. Staking is common in Proof-of-Stake blockchains like Ethereum 2.0 and Cardano.

Liquidity Pools: Liquidity pools are another popular feature of DeFi platforms. Users provide liquidity by depositing their tokens into a pool that supports decentralized trading on the platform. In return, they receive a portion of the trading fees generated by the pool.

NFTs as an Investment

Non-Fungible Tokens (NFTs) have taken the world by storm, representing a new way to own and trade digital assets. Unlike cryptocurrencies such as Bitcoin or Ethereum, NFTs are unique digital tokens that represent ownership of a specific item, such as artwork, music, or virtual real estate.

NFTs are digital certificates of ownership stored on a blockchain: because they are unique (or non-fungible), they cannot be exchanged on a one-to-one basis like Bitcoin or other cryptocurrencies. This makes them perfect for representing ownership of unique assets, from digital art to in-game items.

Examples of NFTs:

- **Digital Art**: Platforms like OpenSea and Rarible allow artists to mint and sell their digital works as NFTs.
- **Music**: Musicians can release songs or albums as

NFTs, granting fans ownership of a one-of-a-kind digital version of the music.

- **Virtual Real Estate**: Projects like Decentraland and The Sandbox allow users to buy, sell, and develop virtual land parcels as NFTs.

NFTs can be a lucrative investment, but they also come with significant risks. The value of an NFT is often driven by factors like rarity, demand, and the reputation of the creator. Some NFTs have sold for millions of dollars, but the market can be speculative and volatile.

Exploring New Frontiers

Advanced crypto concepts like margin trading, DeFi, and NFTs open up exciting opportunities for those looking to go beyond basic trading and investing. However, these strategies also come with added risks, making it crucial to approach them carefully and with a deep understanding of the potential downsides.

Whether you're interested in yield farming, staking, or exploring the world of NFTs, the key is to do thorough research and always have a solid risk management strategy in place.

Conclusion

As you embark on your cryptocurrency journey, the most important advice to keep in mind is to start small and grow steadily. The crypto market can be thrilling, but it's also volatile, and diving in headfirst without caution can lead to unnecessary risk. Begin with modest investments, gradually build your portfolio, and focus on learning as you go.

Recap of Key Points

Throughout this book, we've covered the essential steps for getting started with cryptocurrency:

1. **Understanding the Basics**: Differentiating between trading and investing and grasping key market concepts like bull and bear markets.

2. **Setting Up Your Accounts**: From choosing a reputable exchange to setting up secure wallets, we've guided you through the practical steps.

3. **Making Your First Crypto Purchase**: We provided a detailed look at how to buy crypto, along with the importance of diversifying your investments.

4. **Risk Management**: Learning how to protect your assets through strategies like stop-loss orders, take-profit levels, and dollar-cost averaging.

5. **Staying Safe**: Recognizing scams and security risks while protecting your investments from fraud.

6. **Advanced Concepts**: We touched on margin trading, DeFi, and NFTs for those looking to explore beyond the basics.

Crypto is a journey—one that requires patience, continuous learning, and a disciplined approach. By starting small, growing steadily, and keeping yourself informed, you'll be well-equipped to navigate the exciting and ever-changing world of cryptocurrency.

If you are keen to continue your education on all things Crypto and stay up-to-date on market trends, send an email to admin@tigresspublishing.com.au and become part of the Crypto Community!

Thank you for reading this book, I truly do hope you learned something new and useful. If you could take a minute or two to leave a review on Amazon, I would be truly appreciative as this helps my book to be seen more by others. Thank you again.

References

Books

Ammous, S. (2018). *The Bitcoin standard: The decentralized alternative to central banking*. Wiley.

Antonopoulos, A. M. (2017). *Mastering Bitcoin: Unlocking digital cryptocurrencies*. O'Reilly Media.

Burniske, C., & Tatar, J. (2017). *Cryptoassets: The innovative investor's guide to Bitcoin and beyond*. McGraw-Hill Education.

Drescher, D. (2017). *Blockchain basics: A non-technical introduction in 25 steps*. Apress.

Diedrich, H. (2016). *Ethereum: Blockchains, digital assets, smart contracts, decentralized autonomous organizations*. Wildfire Publishing.

Websites

CoinGecko. (n.d.). *CoinGecko*.

CoinMarketCap. (n.d.). *CoinMarketCap*.

Binance Academy. (n.d.). *Binance Academy*. https://academy.binance.com

Investopedia. (n.d.). *Cryptocurrency section*. https://www.investopedia.com/cryptocurrency-4427699

DeFi Pulse. (n.d.). *DeFi Pulse*.

"Journal of cryptocurrency." (n.d.). *Journal of Cryptocurrency*.

YouTube Channels

Antonopoulos, A. M. (n.d.). *Andreas M. Antonopoulos YouTube channel.*

Coin Bureau. (n.d.). *Coin Bureau YouTube channel.*

DataDash. (n.d.). *DataDash YouTube channel.*

Casey, C. (n.d.). *Crypto Casey YouTube channel.*

Podcasts

Shin, L. (Host). (n.d.). *Unchained Podcast.*

Pompliano, A. (Host). (n.d.). *The Pomp Podcast.* https://anthonypompliano.com/podcast/

Decrypt. (n.d.). *The Decrypt Daily Podcast.* https://decrypt.co/category/podcasts

Made in the USA
Monee, IL
31 July 2025

22306761R00079